THE FUN FILLED FOOTBALL ACTIVITY BOOK FOR KIDS: OVERTIME

IF YOU ENJOY THIS BOOK, CHECK OUT OUR OTHER SPORTS ACTIVITY BOOKS ON AMAZON

LANGSTON PUBLICATIONS

D1607209

THIS BOOK
BELONGS TO

. . . .

BOOK CONTENTS

FOOTBALL TERMS #1

HOW MANY OF THESE FOOTBALL TERMS CAN YOU FIND IN THE WORD SEARCH?

```
C D Z F U U Y Y B R S Z G O J E S
Y K H V V A F M V P M B Z N C T C
P W X A F W O Z W V B J F Y Y T U
Z Q B U I S E H C U S Z E M W C E
P F D Z E N H N R B W H C Z Z Z W
H W Q D L S G A D X B Z O K H T C
I X J E D B L I T Z N Z U T X U Z
U Y G A G N H P F F O M N T H D Y
K C O D O G T Q B R G N T O G T R
H U E B A J U D M U E Z E G B B I
B A B A L L C A R R I E R R M S S
I V I L N R A P R E X U K V U I R
Q F T L C H E C K D O W N I B H M
J Y L S M O S T A B W B L O C K C
B W G Y J A V Y S S C R E Z M K J
R Z Q P L W R E P A K A I U W C V
X Z N I V T Y Y R N K H S M A Z P
```

BALL CARRIER	COUNTER	FIELD GOAL
BLITZ	COVER	FREE KICK
BLOCK	DEAD BALL	GUARD
CHECKDOWN	END ZONE	HAIL MARY

FOOTBALL COLORING #1

COLOR IN THE IMAGE TO BRING IT TO LIFE

WHO AM I?

CAN YOU USE THESE CLUES TO FIGURE OUT WHO THE MYSTERY FOOTBALL PLAYER IS?

ANSWER ON PAGE 65

1) I HAVE WON THE SUPER BOWL MORE TIMES THAN ANY OTHER PLAYER

2) I SIGNED WITH THE TAMPA BAY BUCCANEERS IN MARCH 2020

3) I WAS FIRST DRAFTED IN THE 6TH ROUND OF THE 2002 NFL DRAFT

I AM:

_____

3

FOOTBALL FACT #1

DID YOU KNOW?

UNTIL THE YEAR 1943, FOOTBALL PLAYERS WERE NOT REQUIRED TO WEAR A HELMET.

COLOR BY MATH

CAN YOU SOLVE THESE MATH SUMS AND COLOR THE IMAGE IN CORRECTLY?

12 - Beige   13 - Blue   14 - Yellow   15 - Orange
16 - Green   17 - Red   18 - Light-blue   19 - Brown

TEAM DESIGN

A NEW FOOTBALL TEAM HAS BEEN MADE BUT IT NEEDS YOUR HELP! CAN YOU DESIGN A JERSEY AND A LOGO FOR THEM?

TEAM NAME:

TEAM JERSEY

TEAM LOGO

CODE CRACKING

USING THE TABLE BELOW CAN YOU DECODE THE NAMES OF THESE FOOTBALL TEAMS?

A	B	C	D	E	F	G	H	I	J	K	L	M	N	O	P	Q	R	S	T	U	V	W	X	Y	Z
Q	T	X	V	B	N	E	R	D	O	Z	C	P	H	L	G	U	I	F	K	A	S	Y	M	W	J

EIBBH TQW GQXZBIF

_____ ___ _____

CQF SBEQF IQDVBIF

___ _____ _____

PDHHBFLKQ SDZDHEF

_____ _____

VBHSBI TILHXLF

_____ _____

FOOTBALL COLORING #2

COLOR IN THE IMAGE TO BRING IT TO LIFE

SOLUTION ON PAGE: 70

CRAZY MAZE

CAN YOU RUN THE BALL THROUGH THE MAZE AND TO THE END ZONE ON THE OTHER SIDE?

START

MAZE 1

END

9

LOGO DESIGN

DESIGN A LOGO FOR YOUR DREAM TEAM USING DIFFERENT
COLORS AND PATTERNS

FOOTBALL FACT #2

DID YOU KNOW?

A 30 SECOND TELEVISION ADVERT DURING THE 2021 SUPERBOWL WOULD COST $5 MILLION.

FOOTBALL COLORING #3

COLOR IN THE IMAGE TO BRING IT TO LIFE

TRIVIA TIME!!

HOW MANY OF THESE TRIVIA QUESTIONS CAN YOU GUESS CORRECTLY?

THIS ROUND IS ALL ABOUT FOOTBALL RULES

ANSWERS ON PAGE 69

QUESTION 1:

HOW MANY POINTS IS A TOUCHDOWN WORTH?

QUESTION 2:

HOW MANY POINTS IS A FIELD GOAL WORTH?

QUESTION 3:

WHAT IS THE NAME FOR THE METHOD OF SCORING WHEN THE BALL CARRIER IS TACKLED IN THEIR OWN END ZONE?

QUESTION 4:

HOW MANY MINUTES LONG ARE PROFESSIONAL FOOTBALL MATCHES?

ANSWERS ON PAGE: 72

MATCH UP MAYHEM

CAN YOU MATCH UP THE PLAYER TO THE YEAR THAT THEY WERE FIRST DRAFTED INTO THE NFL?

ODELL BECKHAM JR.   2000

TOM BRADY   2017

JOE BURROW   2020

ROB GRONKOWSKI   2014

PATRICK MAHOMES II   2010

14

FOOTBALL FACT #3

DID YOU KNOW?

CHICAGO BEARS' STADIUM, SOLDIER FIELD, IS THE OLDEST NFL STADIUM AND HAS BEEN OPEN SINCE 1924.

FOOTBALL COLORING #4

COLOR IN THE IMAGE TO BRING IT TO LIFE

FOOTBALL ANAGRAMS

CAN YOU UNSCRAMBLE THESE ANAGRAMS TO WORK OUT WHICH FOOTBALL STADIUM SHOULD BE MADE UP OF THE LETTERS?

ALBAEMU EDIFL

------- -----

FSIO IUDSMAT

---- -------

DCEMREES ZNBE PSDUERMEO

-------- ---- ---------

TNIAGELLA ASMIDTU

TEAM DESIGN

A NEW FOOTBALL TEAM HAS BEEN MADE BUT IT NEEDS YOUR HELP! CAN YOU DESIGN A JERSEY AND A LOGO FOR THEM?

TEAM NAME:

TEAM JERSEY

TEAM LOGO

FOOTBALL FACT #4

DID YOU KNOW?

THE GREEN BAY PACKERS ARE THE ONLY NON-PROFIT AND PUBLICLY OWNED TEAM IN THE NFL.

WHO AM I?

CAN YOU USE THESE CLUES TO FIGURE OUT WHO THE MYSTERY FOOTBALL PLAYER IS?

ANSWER ON PAGE 66

1) I WAS THE FIRST OVERALL PICK OF THE 1998 NFL DRAFT

2) I PLAYED FOR THE INDIANAPOLIS COLTS BETWEEN 1998 AND 2011

3) SUPER BOWL XLI (41) WAS MY FIRST SUPER BOWL WIN

I AM:

_____

20

FOOTBALL LEGENDS

HOW MANY OF THESE FOOTBALL LEGENDS CAN YOU FIND IN THE WORD SEARCH?

```
K J R Q H U H X I X U L J E F N T
Y U R J N O D Z C L Q K N A A J T
R K W F A I B K X X J J N A L M A
P Y R I X U N Q F I R N V W U C P
N V R O Y M P P Z P Q T Q O L F Y
M K S B R K M T A U P I O V Z K X
C B P A G B R A D Y X N Q U M R M
C J H E N T Z Y N Q T X M O I L S
D O N A L D K L F N S O F I Z C M
F B W H I T E O N P I E N J Q X O
D Z R O D G E R S M O N T A N A T
P P I A M L O P S F C Y G I T Q W
B W C S V K M N O A X H U O P Q Z
A R E X L I S D V E F U T K X K G
T T O Y I N Y C E R M E O S S S W
Z L E W I S Y F C A X L Y S A N P
Q S C Q N Q Q O A Q G C A X T T W
```

BRADY	MANNING	RODGERS
BROWN	MONTANA	SANDERS
DONALD	PAYTON	TAYLOR
LEWIS	RICE	WHITE

21

FOOTBALL COLORING #5

COLOR IN THE IMAGE TO BRING IT TO LIFE

CODE CRACKING

USING THE TABLE BELOW CAN YOU DECODE THE NAMES OF THESE FOOTBALL COACHES?

A	B	C	D	E	F	G	H	I	J	K	L	M	N	O	P	Q	R	S	T	U	V	W	X	Y	Z
Q	T	X	V	B	N	E	R	D	O	Z	C	P	H	L	G	U	I	F	K	A	S	Y	M	W	J

OLRH RQITQAER

____ _____

FBQH PXSQW

____ _____

TDCC TBCDXRDXZ

____ _____

QHVW IBDV

____ ____

23

LOGO DESIGN

DESIGN A LOGO FOR YOUR DREAM TEAM USING DIFFERENT
COLORS AND PATTERNS

FOOTBALL FACT #5

DID YOU
KNOW?

THE NFL IS THE WORLD'S
RICHEST PROFESSIONAL
SPORTS LEAGUE.

PERFECT PLAYER

BUILD YOUR PERFECT PLAYER BY USING ELEMENTS OF ALL THE BEST
FOOTBALL PLAYERS E.G. BRADY'S THROWING OR TYREEK HILL'S SPEED

FOOTBALL BRAIN: _____

POWER: _____

THROWING: _____

CATCHING: _____

KICKING: _____

SPEED: _____

26

COLOR BY MATH

CAN YOU SOLVE THESE MATH SUMS AND COLOR THE IMAGE IN CORRECTLY?

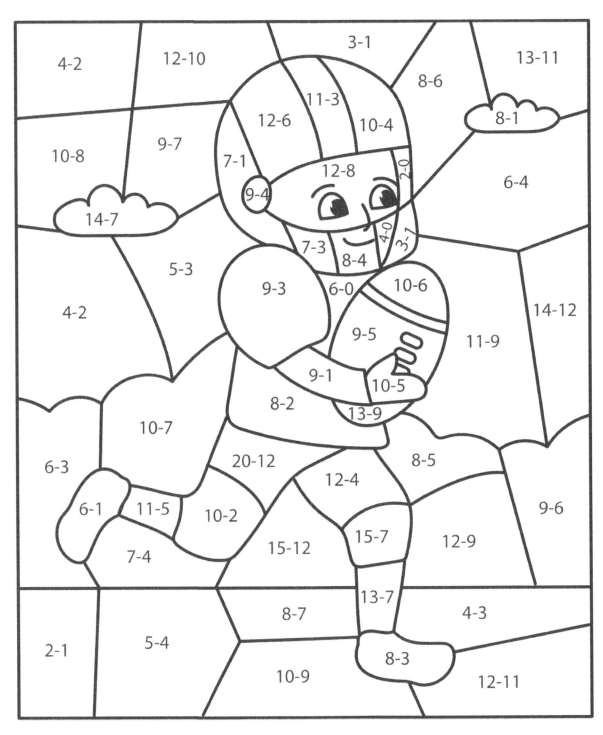

1 - Green   2 - Blue   3 - Light-green   4 - Brown
5 - Black   6 - Red   7 - Light-blue   8 - Orange

ANSWERS ON PAGE: 71

CODE CRACKING

USING THE TABLE BELOW CAN YOU DECODE THE NAMES OF THESE FOOTBALL MASCOTS?

A	B	C	D	E	F	G	H	I	J	K	L	M	N	O	P	Q	R	S	T	U	V	W	X	Y	Z
Q	T	X	V	B	N	E	R	D	O	Z	C	P	H	L	G	U	I	F	K	A	S	Y	M	W	J

XQGKQDH NBQI

_____ ____

FDI GAII

___ ____

FKQCBW VQ TBQI

_____ __ ____

YRL VBW

___ ___

28

FOOTBALL FACT #6

DID YOU KNOW?

TOM BRADY HAS WON MORE SUPER BOWLS THAN ANY OTHER PLAYER OR TEAM.

FOOTBALL COLORING #6

COLOR IN THE IMAGE TO BRING IT TO LIFE

SOLUTION ON PAGE: 70

CRAZY MAZE

CAN YOU RUN THE BALL THROUGH THE MAZE AND TO THE END ZONE
ON THE OTHER SIDE?

START

MAZE 2

END

MATCH UP MAYHEM

CAN YOU MATCH UP THE PLAYER TO THE POSITION THAT THEY PLAY?

DAVANTE ADAMS   CENTER

TRENT WILLIAMS   DEFENSIVE TACKLE

AARON RODGERS   OFFENSIVE TACKLE

AARON DONALD   WIDE RECEIVER

RODNEY HUDSON   QUARTERBACK

TEAM DESIGN

A NEW FOOTBALL TEAM HAS BEEN MADE BUT IT NEEDS YOUR HELP! CAN YOU DESIGN A JERSEY AND A LOGO FOR THEM?

TEAM NAME:

TEAM JERSEY

TEAM LOGO

FOOTBALL FACT #7

DID YOU KNOW?

IT TAKES 3,000 COWS TO SUPPLY THE NFL WITH A YEAR'S WORTH OF FOOTBALLS.

FOOTBALL COLORING #7

COLOR IN THE IMAGE TO BRING IT TO LIFE

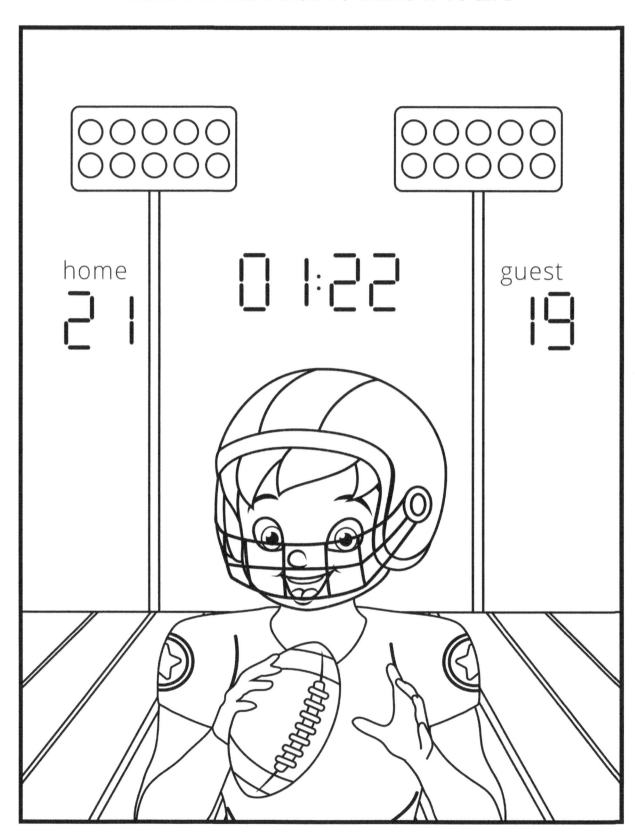

FOOTBALL ANAGRAMS

CAN YOU UNSCRAMBLE THESE ANAGRAMS TO WORK OUT WHICH FOOTBALL TEAM SHOULD BE MADE UP OF THE LETTERS?

INACINCTNI ENGASBL

---------- -------

RVEEND COBRNSO

------ -------

BPGIRUHSTT ERTSSEEL

---------- --------

FABOUFL LILBS

------- -----

TRIVIA TIME!!

HOW MANY OF THESE TRIVIA QUESTIONS CAN YOU GUESS CORRECTLY?

THIS ROUND IS ALL ABOUT THE SUPER BOWL

ANSWERS ON PAGE 69

QUESTION 1:

WHO WON THE 2022 SUPER BOWL?

QUESTION 2:

IN WHICH MONTH WAS THE SUPER BOWL ORIGINALLY PLAYED?

QUESTION 3:

WHICH TEAM WON THE FIRST EVER SUPER BOWL IN 1967?

QUESTION 4:

IN WHICH STATE WAS THE 2022 SUPER BOWL PLAYED?

FOOTBALL FACT #8

DID YOU KNOW?

PLAYERS' NAMES WERE NOT PUT ON THE BACK OF THEIR JERSEYS UNTIL THE 1960S.

FOOTBALL ANAGRAMS

CAN YOU UNSCRAMBLE THESE ANAGRAMS TO WORK OUT WHICH FOOTBALL PLAYER SHOULD BE MADE UP OF THE LETTERS?

CARIPKT EMAMHOS

_____ _____

LSEMY TAGRRET

_____ _____

OORCEP PUKP

_____ ____

OJE RUBOWR

___ _____

WHO AM I?

CAN YOU USE THESE CLUES TO FIGURE OUT WHO THE MYSTERY FOOTBALL PLAYER IS?

ANSWER ON PAGE 67

1) I PLAYED FOR THE SAN FRANCISCO 49ERS BETWEEN 2011 AND 2016

2) I REFUSED TO STAND DURING THE NATIONAL ANTHEM IN 2016

3) I WAS A STAR IN NIKE'S 'DREAM CRAZY' AD CAMPAIGN

I AM:

_____

FOOTBALL FACT #9

DID YOU KNOW?

CHICAGO BEARS, MIAMI DOLPHINS AND THE NEW ENGLAND PATRIOTS ARE THE ONLY TEAMS TO BE UNBEATEN IN A SEASON.

FOOTBALL COLORING #8

COLOR IN THE IMAGE TO BRING IT TO LIFE

SOLUTION ON PAGE: 70

CRAZY MAZE

CAN YOU RUN THE BALL THROUGH THE MAZE AND TO THE END ZONE ON THE OTHER SIDE?

START

MAZE 3

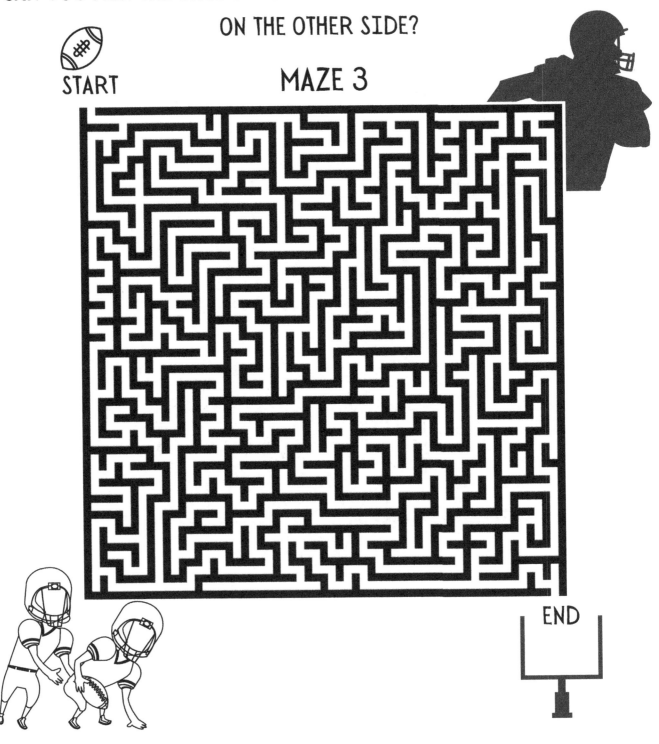

END

43

TEAM DESIGN

A NEW FOOTBALL TEAM HAS BEEN MADE BUT IT NEEDS YOUR HELP! CAN YOU DESIGN A JERSEY AND A LOGO FOR THEM?

TEAM NAME:

_____

TEAM JERSEY

TEAM LOGO

MATCH UP MAYHEM

CAN YOU MATCH UP THE TEAM TO THE NAME OF THEIR MASCOT?

TENNESSEE TITANS   ROWDY

DETROIT LIONS   BLITZ

CLEVELAND BROWNS   T-RAC

DALLAS COWBOYS   CHOMPS

SEATTLE SEAHAWKS   ROARY

FOOTBALL FACT #10

DID YOU KNOW?

THE NFL IS SPLIT INTO
TWO DIVISIONS: THE NFC
AND THE AFC. IN TOTAL,
THERE ARE 32 TEAMS.

COLOR BY MATH

CAN YOU SOLVE THESE MATH SUMS AND COLOR THE IMAGE IN CORRECTLY?

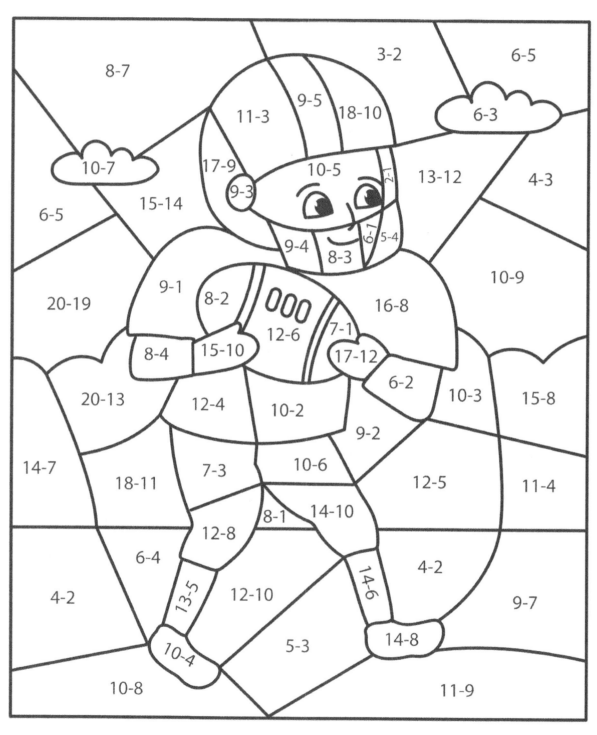

1 - Blue   2 - Green   3 - Light-blue   4 - Red
5 - Beige   6 - Brown   7 - Light-green   8 - Yellow

LOGO DESIGN

DESIGN A LOGO FOR YOUR DREAM TEAM USING DIFFERENT
COLORS AND PATTERNS

FOOTBALL FACT #11

DID YOU KNOW?

THE HOME TEAM IS REQUIRED TO SUPPLY 24 FOOTBALLS FOR A MATCH.

WHO AM I?

CAN YOU USE THESE CLUES TO FIGURE OUT WHO THE MYSTERY FOOTBALL PLAYER IS?

ANSWER ON PAGE 68

1) I MOVED TO THE LA RAMS FROM THE CLEVELAND BROWNS

2) PEOPLE OFTEN CALL ME BY MY NICKNAME WHICH IS OBJ

3) IN 2017 I SIGNED A DEAL WITH NIKE WORTH $25 MILLION

I AM:

_____

TRIVIA TIME!!

HOW MANY OF THESE TRIVIA QUESTIONS CAN YOU GUESS CORRECTLY?

THIS ROUND IS ALL ABOUT TOM BRADY

ANSWERS ON PAGE 69

QUESTION 1:

TOM BRADY WAS KNOWN FOR PLAYING IN WHICH POSITION?

QUESTION 2:

HOW MANY SUPER BOWLS HAS TOM BRADY WON? (AS OF 2022)

QUESTION 3:

WHICH TEAM DID TOM BRADY SPEND MOST OF HIS CAREER PLAYING FOR?

QUESTION 4:

IN WHAT YEAR WAS TOM BRADY FIRST DRAFTED?

FOOTBALL FACT #12

DID YOU KNOW?

THERE ARE SEVEN OFFICIALS PRESENT DURING A FOOTBALL MATCH.

FOOTBALL COLORING #9

COLOR IN THE IMAGE TO BRING IT TO LIFE

SOLUTION ON PAGE: 70

CRAZY MAZE

CAN YOU RUN THE BALL THROUGH THE MAZE AND TO THE END ZONE
ON THE OTHER SIDE?

START

MAZE 4

END

54

FOOTBALL TERMS #2

HOW MANY OF THESE FOOTBALL TERMS CAN YOU FIND IN THE WORD SEARCH?

```
K H L F O Q M R Z Z O J H C V Y A
F W A I M S E K E M U S C G E K P
V M T N N M W J V I T X W M M I K
D H O L D E R H O E P N A X J H E
G T U F T O M Y J L U P Y N U Q Y
O F C X F D F A P W S X W B Q L O
C P H W P S X F N D E S D B O U N
L R D X J L I W J R Q P K Q W I N
O G O J S A C D R M V I F S I Q R
L G W L D N I I E B K A A M F H P
U Y N N P T E G V S O Q P L T J A
L H S D L O F A E F R F K D H H C
O G D N G X C N R V S X V B L Q K
B B V U S T X K S A F E T Y A J A
G P U L K I C K E R Z P O O J X G
Z E I N B Q U A R T E R E V W Q E
P V H K U K E Q K P K N K O W W Y
```

HAND OFF	OFFSIDE	REVERSE
HOLDER	PACKAGE	SAFETY
KICKER	POCKET	SLANT
LINEMAN	QUARTER	TOUCHDOWN

CODE CRACKING

USING THE TABLE BELOW CAN YOU DECODE THE NAMES OF THESE FOOTBALL OFFICIALS?

A	B	C	D	E	F	G	H	I	J	K	L	M	N	O	P	Q	R	S	T	U	V	W	X	Y	Z
Q	T	X	V	B	N	E	R	D	O	Z	C	P	H	L	G	U	I	F	K	A	S	Y	M	W	J

VLYH OAVEB

____ _____

APGDIB

_____

IBNBIBB

_____

CDHB OAVEB

____ _____

FOOTBALL FACT #13

DID YOU KNOW?

THE GREEN BAY PACKERS WON THE FIRST SUPER BOWL IN 1967. THE FINAL WAS HELD IN LOS ANGELES.

MATCH UP MAYHEM

CAN YOU MATCH UP THE TEAM TO THEIR MAIN HOME KIT COLORS?

NEW YORK GIANTS	BLUE + YELLOW
KANSAS CITY CHIEFS	RED + WHITE
NEW ORLEANS SAINTS	BLUE + WHITE
GREEN BAY PACKERS	BLACK + GOLD
LOS ANGELES RAMS	GREEN + YELLOW

FOOTBALL COLORING #10

COLOR IN THE IMAGE TO BRING IT TO LIFE

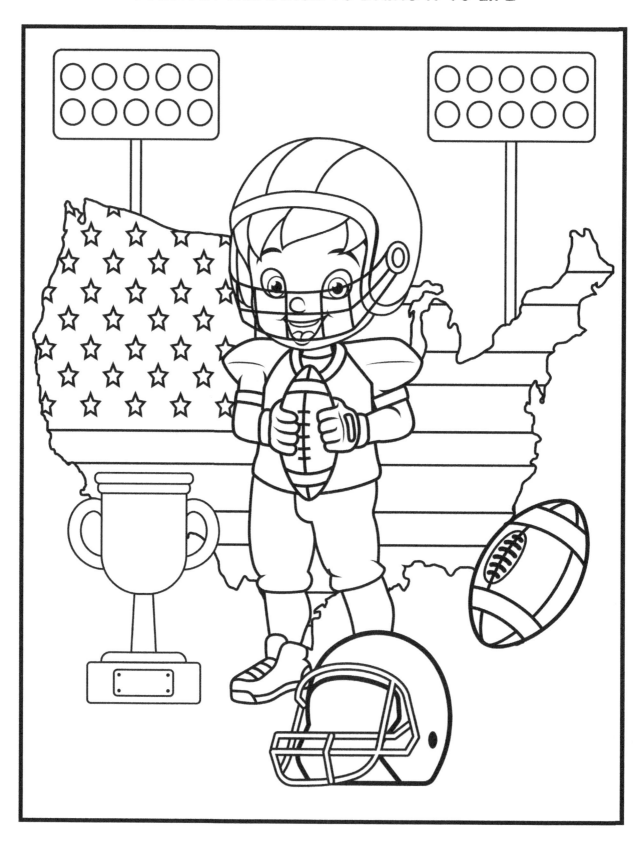

FOOTBALL ANAGRAMS

CAN YOU UNSCRAMBLE THESE ANAGRAMS TO WORK OUT WHICH FOOTBALL POSITION SHOULD BE MADE UP OF THE LETTERS?

HGTTI NED

----- ---

IDMLED ABCRKIENLE

------- ----------

AFLULBKC

KCRIEK

FOOTBALL FACT #14

DID YOU KNOW?

19 OUT OF 20 OF THE MOST WATCHED TELEVISION EVENTS IN AMERICA HAVE BEEN SUPER BOWL MATCHES.

COLOR BY MATH

CAN YOU SOLVE THESE MATH SUMS AND COLOR THE IMAGE IN CORRECTLY?

10 - Light-green   11 - Green   12 - Beige   13 - Red
14 - Blue   15 - Yellow   16 - Brown   17 - Light-blue

FOOTBALL FACT #15

DID YOU KNOW?

FOOTBALL HAS ONE OF THE SHORTEST SEASONS OF ANY PROFESSIONAL SPORT, LASTING JUST 17 WEEKS.

ANSWERS

IT'S TIME TO SEE HOW MANY
QUESTIONS/SOLUTIONS YOU
GOT CORRECT

WHO AM I?

CAN YOU USE THESE CLUES TO FIGURE OUT WHO THE MYSTERY FOOTBALL PLAYER IS?

1) I HAVE WON THE SUPER BOWL MORE TIMES THAN ANY OTHER PLAYER

2) I SIGNED WITH THE TAMPA BAY BUCCANEERS IN MARCH 2020

3) I WAS FIRST DRAFTED IN THE 6TH ROUND OF THE 2002 NFL DRAFT

I AM:

TOM BRADY

WHO AM I?

CAN YOU USE THESE CLUES TO FIGURE OUT WHO THE
MYSTERY FOOTBALL PLAYER IS?

1) I WAS THE FIRST
OVERALL PICK OF THE
1998 NFL DRAFT

2) I PLAYED FOR THE
INDIANAPOLIS COLTS
BETWEEN 1998 AND 2011

3) SUPER BOWL XLI (41)
WAS MY FIRST SUPER
BOWL WIN

I AM:
PEYTON MANNING

WHO AM I?

CAN YOU USE THESE CLUES TO FIGURE OUT WHO THE MYSTERY FOOTBALL PLAYER IS?

1) I PLAYED FOR THE SAN FRANCISCO 49ERS BETWEEN 2011 AND 2016

2) I REFUSED TO STAND DURING THE NATIONAL ANTHEM IN 2016

3) I WAS A STAR IN NIKE'S 'DREAM CRAZY' AD CAMPAIGN

I AM:
COLIN KAEPERNICK

WHO AM I?

CAN YOU USE THESE CLUES TO FIGURE OUT WHO THE
MYSTERY FOOTBALL PLAYER IS?

1) I MOVED TO THE LA
RAMS FROM THE
CLEVELAND BROWNS

2) PEOPLE OFTEN CALL ME
BY MY NICKNAME WHICH
IS OBJ

3) IN 2017 I SIGNED A
DEAL WITH NIKE WORTH
$25 MILLION

I AM:
ODELL BECKHAM JR

68

ANSWER PAGE

ROUND 1 - RULES

QUESTION 1:
HOW MANY POINTS IS A TOUCHDOWN WORTH?
ANSWER: 6 POINTS

QUESTION 2:
HOW MANY POINTS IS A FIELD GOAL WORTH?
ANSWER: 3 POINTS

QUESTION 3:
WHAT IS THE NAME FOR THE METHOD OF SCORING WHEN THE BALL
CARRIER IS TACKLED IN THEIR OWN END ZONE?
ANSWER: A SAFETY

QUESTION 4:
HOW MANY MINUTES LONG ARE PROFESSIONAL FOOTBALL MATCHES?
ANSWER: 60 MINUTES

ROUND 2 - THE SUPER BOWL

QUESTION 1:
WHO WON THE 2022 SUPER BOWL?
ANSWER: LOS ANGELES RAMS

QUESTION 2:
IN WHICH MONTH WAS THE SUPER BOWL ORIGINALLY PLAYED?
ANSWER: JANUARY

QUESTION 3:
WHICH TEAM WON THE FIRST EVER SUPER BOWL IN 1967?
ANSWER: GREEN BAY PACKERS

QUESTION 4:
IN WHICH STATE WAS THE 2022 SUPER BOWL PLAYED?
ANSWER: CALIFORNIA

ROUND 3 - TOM BRADY

QUESTION 1:
TOM BRADY WAS KNOWN FOR PLAYING IN WHICH POSITION?
ANSWER: QUARTERBACK

QUESTION 2:
HOW MANY SUPER BOWLS HAS TOM BRADY WON? (AS OF 2022)
ANSWER: 7

QUESTION 3:
WHICH TEAM DID TOM BRADY SPEND MOST OF HIS CAREER PLAYING
FOR?
ANSWER: NEW ENGLAND PATRIOTS

QUESTION 4:
IN WHAT YEAR WAS TOM BRADY FIRST DRAFTED?
ANSWER: 2000

CRAZY MAZE

ANSWER PAGE

MAZE 1

MAZE 2

MAZE 3

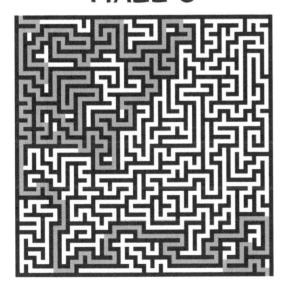

MAZE 4

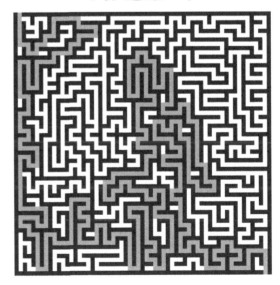

CODE CRACKING

ANSWER PAGE

FOOTBALL TEAMS

EIBBH TQW GQXZBIF
GREEN BAY PACKERS

CQF SBEQF IQOVBIF
LAS VEGAS RAIDERS

PDHHBFLKQ SDZDHEF
MINNESOTA VIKINGS

VBHSBI TILHXLF
DENVER BRONCOS

FOOTBALL COACHES

OLRH RQITQAER
JOHN HARBAUGH

FBQH PXSQW
SEAN MCVAY

TDCC TBCDXRDXZ
BILL BELICHICK

QHVW IBDV
ANDY REID

FOOTBALL MASCOTS

XQGKQDH NBQI
CAPTAIN FEAR

FDI GAII
SIR PURR

FKQCBW VQ TBQI
STALEY DA BEAR

YRL VBW
WHO DEY

FOOTBALL OFFICIALS

VLYH OAVEB
DOWN JUDGE

APGDIB
UMPIRE

IBNBIBB
REFEREE

CDHB OAVEB
LINE JUDGE

MATCH UP MAYHEM

CAN YOU MATCH UP THE PLAYER TO THE YEAR THAT THEY WERE
FIRST DRAFTED INTO THE NFL

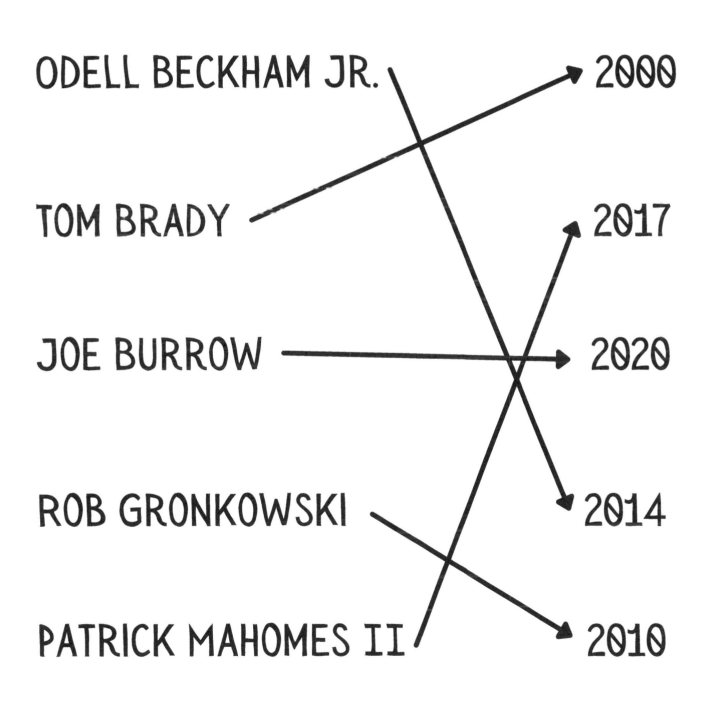

ODELL BECKHAM JR.

TOM BRADY

JOE BURROW

ROB GRONKOWSKI

PATRICK MAHOMES II

2000

2017

2020

2014

2010

MATCH UP MAYHEM

CAN YOU MATCH UP THE PLAYER TO THEIR CORRECT PLAYING POSITION?

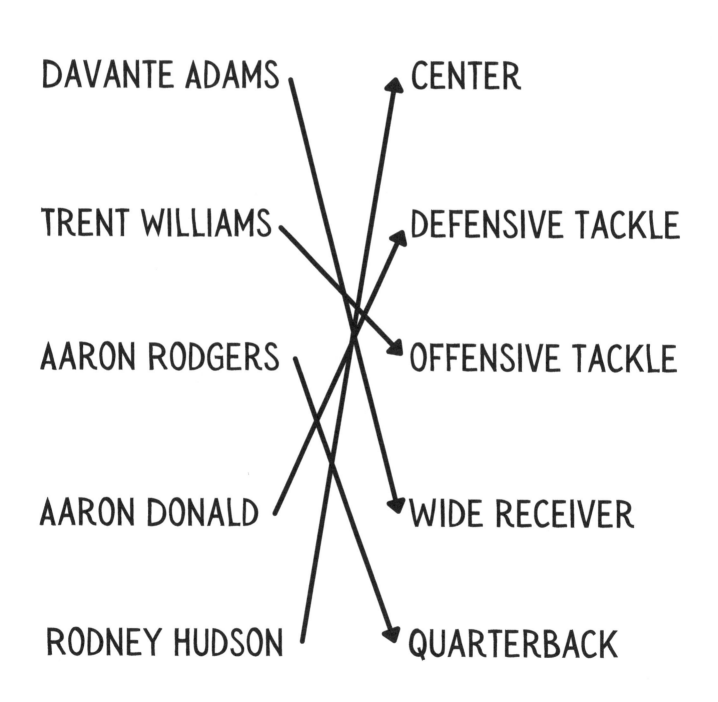

DAVANTE ADAMS

TRENT WILLIAMS

AARON RODGERS

AARON DONALD

RODNEY HUDSON

CENTER

DEFENSIVE TACKLE

OFFENSIVE TACKLE

WIDE RECEIVER

QUARTERBACK

MATCH UP MAYHEM

CAN YOU MATCH UP THE TEAM WITH THEIR MASCOT?

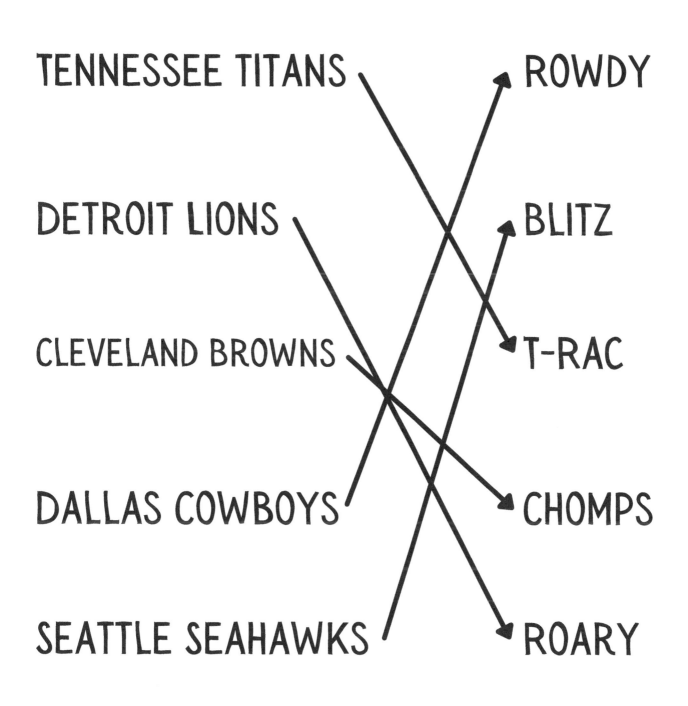

TENNESSEE TITANS

DETROIT LIONS

CLEVELAND BROWNS

DALLAS COWBOYS

SEATTLE SEAHAWKS

ROWDY

BLITZ

T-RAC

CHOMPS

ROARY

MATCH UP MAYHEM

CAN YOU MATCH UP THE TEAM WITH THEIR MAIN HOME KIT COLORS?

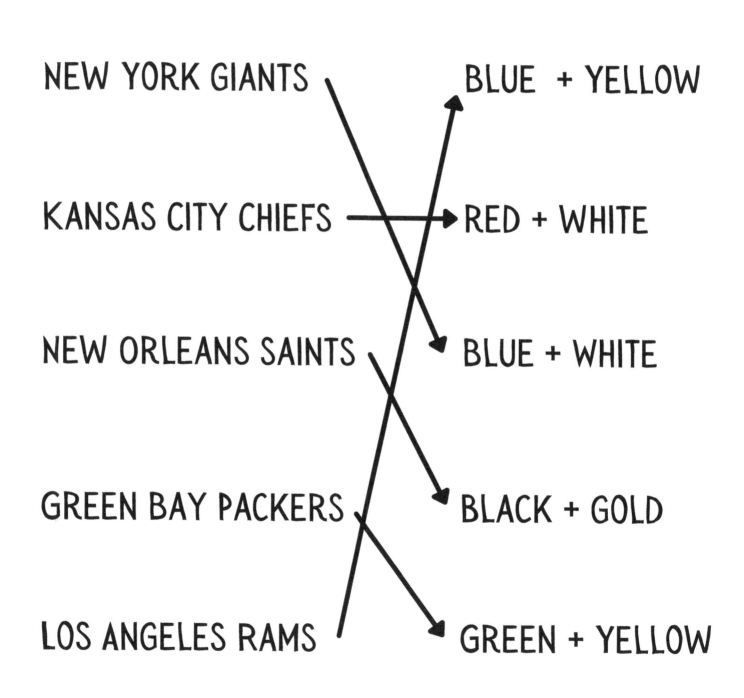

NEW YORK GIANTS   BLUE + YELLOW

KANSAS CITY CHIEFS   RED + WHITE

NEW ORLEANS SAINTS   BLUE + WHITE

GREEN BAY PACKERS   BLACK + GOLD

LOS ANGELES RAMS   GREEN + YELLOW

FOOTBALL ANAGRAMS

ANSWER PAGE

STADIUMS

ALBAEMU EDIFL
LAMBEAU FIELD

FSIO IUDSMAT
SOFI STADIUM

DCEMREES ZNBE PSDUERMEO
MERCEDES BENZ SUPERDOME

TNIAGELLA ASMIDTU
ALLEGIANT STADIUM

TEAMS

INACINCTNI ENGASBL
CINCINNATI BENGALS

RVEEND COBRNSO
DENVER BRONCOS

BPGIRUHSTT ERTSSEEL
PITTSBURGH STEELERS

FABOUFL LILBS
BUFFALO BILLS

PLAYERS

CARIPKT EMAMHOS
PATRICK MAHOMES

LSEMY TAGRRET
MYLES GARRETT

OORCEP PUKP
COOPER KUPP

OJE RUBOWR
JOE BURROW

POSITIONS

HGTTI NED
TIGHT END

IDMLED ABCRKIENLE
MIDDLE LINEBACKER

AFLULBKC
FULLBACK

KCRIEK
KICKER

WORD SEARCHES

ANSWER PAGE

FOOTBALL TERMS #1

FOOTBALL LEGENDS

FOOTBALL TERMS #2

77

Made in the USA
Middletown, DE
18 September 2022

10701082R00046